Norman Goldstein

THE BOOK
OF
NORMANISMS

Adages and pictorial visions to provide a
fresh perspective on daily living

Momentous Publications, Inc.

Cover design by Jevgenija Bitter
Illustrations by Rachel Caruana
Typesetting by Sadie Butterworth-Jones

Printed by IngramSpark

ISBN 978-0-578-80572-6

ABOUT THE AUTHOR

From an early age, I experienced difficulties in absorbing the meaning from written words. Struggling to comprehend complex sentences was extremely uncomfortable. I became a dreamer and a fantasizer to gain knowledge and understanding of concepts being expressed. This process went on for decades unknowingly.

In my mid-thirties, one of my children was diagnosed with hyperactivity and ADHD. I was also tested to determine if it was hereditary. I found out that I did have ADHD. This realization explained a lot of my difficulties in understanding literature. I began to realize that I was using metaphors, analogies, and visual stories to communicate to people. This experiential, self-taught process also helped me to have a deeper understanding of my life and the life of others.

As time went on, and daily events would occur, I begin seeing short story clips develop in my mind. Ultimately, I started talking in visual metaphors to express myself with multi-dimensional clarity. They have been a key tool in helping me grasp and digest some of life's most common and difficult issues. Typically, the ones that are most often the hardest to find peace with.

I had the desire to give back to my community and trained to be a mediator and an arbitrator. I am also a business coach and a mentor to those in need of guidance and hope. Friends and family have encouraged me over the years to provide my visual story telling skills and guidance to those who yearn for a better understanding of life's journey. I have been honored by being selected as a Congressional Leadership Award recipient, recognition by CNN for changing lives in America and A Global Goodwill Ambassador and Humanitarian.

As often happens, people suggested I write a book about my visional metaphors. Writing a book appeared to be a daunting task. In lieu of doing a book, I developed a website, *coachnorm.com* for my coaching work and began posting my visual thoughts. During the 2020 pandemic a friend, Sarah, offered to help create a book using my visual thoughts and engage an artist to create complementary illustrations. At last, *The Book of Normanisms* was born.

ACKNOWLEDGMENTS

This first edition is an amalgamation of many years of self-reflection, discovery and then renovation. Most importantly, during my journey on this planet, it has been numerous human encounters, both pleasurable and painful, that enabled and influenced my thinking. I am truly blessed, in hindsight, that those harsh instances reshaped the way I now view my reality.

I would like to mention a mentee of mine, Barry Wecker, who suggested more than thirty years ago that I write down some of the sayings I presented to him as examples of the way I view my world. His passing from lung cancer was a profound time and caused me to reflect on the meaning of human intimacy, unbeknownst and unknown to me.

My spiritual mentor, Tom Skinner, provided a vision of how "good always comes from the bad." His guidance and wisdom enabled me to "sit loose in the saddle of life," as my world bucks and kicks through its daily routine.

Dr. Richard Carlson, whose "don't sweat the small stuff" and his simple grasp of complex issues offered an ease on this voyage of life even through the roughest of seas.

My wife Marci, whose undying commitment, patience and love provide me with the basis for a life beyond my wildest dreams.

Finally, to our illustrator, Rachel Caruana from Malta, whose tireless effort brought these sayings to life, and to Sarah Martin, based in the UK, who assisted in amassing these writings into a book that finally came to life... my deepest gratitude to you all.

Now your journey begins....

Letting go of resentment, hostility and angry feelings is difficult. A child's straw finger toy is an example of how we can free ourselves of them. The harder we struggle, the less likely we can be free from these emotions. Relax and enjoy your freedom.

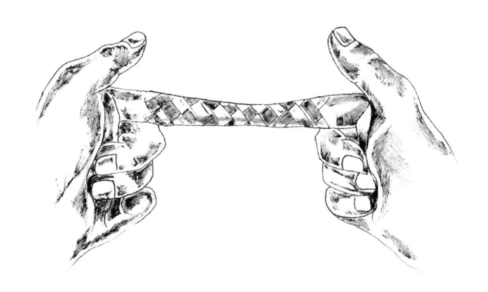

Truly loving someone is keeping their vulnerabilities locked away, even when you a have a disagreement.

Things that happen to us can either be life-threatening or ego-threatening. If it is life-threatening, move at light speed. If its ego-threatening, let it go. It is not worth the cost to our emotional and spiritual currency to defend our egos.

An intelligent person knows what they do know and knows what they don't know. A wise person is always open to seeking help and guidance to improve on the quality and quantity of their knowledge.

I must be responsible for my actions. This way I can't blame what happens to me on a mysterious force outside my control. Then followed up by the victim role and the "poor me's".

In business, make everyone feel like they are sitting on the same side of the table, rather than across from you.

Our eyes are optical monitors into our souls.

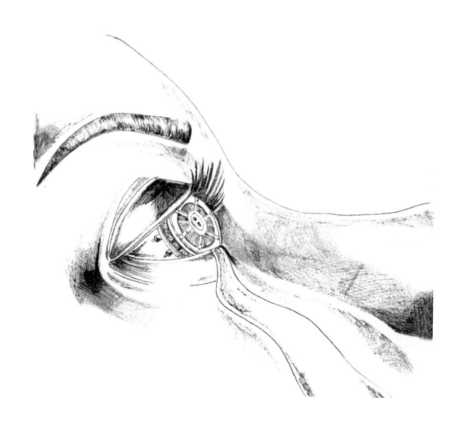

The glass is neither half full nor half empty. It is always overflowing with opportunity. Our job is to look for the possibilities in the overflow.

We need to ask others for what we need and want. It is frustrating when we expect them to be a mind reader.

We human beings are all created equal. We are all but a stitch in the fabric of humanity. The stitches around you must be strong and durable to withstand the elements throughout your life.

Our greatest challenge in life is to get our insides to match with our outsides. The work has to begin on the inside.

As part of life, highly-charged and emotional events will occur. In any 24-hour period we can deal with whatever situations occur. We should work towards staying in the present moment versus projecting about emotional outcomes. We generate adrenaline when getting highly charged, and the anxiety, fear and worry can distort our perception about the situation. Staying present and emotionally balanced offers the best possibility to make sound and prudent decisions.

I hadn't noticed that you were appointed by some high court to judge another human's behavior. Remember those who judge and gossip don't matter; those who matter don't judge and gossip.

Use words like: "I can," "I will," and "I know," instead of words like: "I don't," "I can't," "I'll never," and "I won't." We don't realize that the use of certain words are programming messages (just like in a computer) to our brain and then our body responds. If we say "I can't," it's like instructing a computer to shut down. If you say "I can," it's like calculating a problem looking for an answer.

Always give your full support to children when they want to try something new. A seemingly silly or insignificant attempt of trying something different may lead to a remarkable direction.

Concert
Tonight

We are creatures of habit. When leaving the convenience of our home surroundings we can subtly but unknowingly lose a sense of comfort and contentment. When leaving your nest, take some twigs and branches with you for self-care in your short-term environment. Photos, meaningful possessions and special books are equally as important as taking vitamins, medicines and cosmetics.

Remember the feeling of taking a trip to a new destination? It always seems longer going than coming back. The same emotion applies to trying something new. If only we could know that trying something new would feel easier once we have tried it.

Choose your words carefully when talking about others. If you talk like garbage you may emit an unpleasant aura.

There are all sorts of opportunities hiding in plain sight around us. We need to adjust our perception of our world to view them. Are you wearing "bemoaning my fate" glasses or "opportunity glasses?"

Sometimes we feel like we are not at our best. In these times, strive to be your best "you". Don't project what you think or feel you could or should be. You are enough being who you are right now.

Fantasizing is a gift of free thought and imagination. Let these thoughts stay as thoughts and end there.

Be careful about spending energy on thinking about how old you are. It is better to think act and feel young. Our brains respond to the thoughts that occupy our mind.

There are many people with different types of handicaps. There are those who do not have special parking spaces but are emotionally or spiritually challenged. Their handicap requires a special compassionate "access ramp" to their soul.

When we are desperate to have something we desire, by trying to grab at it, we push it further away. Our desperation moves it out of reach by rippling the emotional waves. Being patient allows the forces of the universe to move it towards us.

We shine from the inside out. It's critical what thoughts we put in our minds.

Humility must be a component in our central ecosystem. It's like having a sprinkler system in a restaurant kitchen. When it gets too hot that little element melts from the heat and the water puts out the fire. Installing a humility system can prevent us from a spiritual and emotional meltdown.

The secret to getting help is to ask for it.

When speaking to people your words should feel like you are rolling out a red carpet for them to come into your home. The words should come from your heart and not from your head.

Life hands us all types of situations. The fact is that we cannot foretell the future results of these occurrences. Over time, these seemingly painful situations can turn out to be great growth opportunities in disguise. Look for the opportunity when adversity comes.

Your health is the most important asset you can protect. Like your car, make certain that you bring yourself in for regular tune-ups. You never want to hear the words, "If you only came in 6 months ago we could have avoided this situation..."

Be a big person in everything you attempt. Making the pie bigger instead of looking for your own slice allows everyone a chance for abundance.

Happiness and joy are a state of mind. It's all about how we think about ourselves in respect to our world. Be mindful of the words used in your daily living.

Having friends or family members whose judgment we trust is invaluable. We must trust those to avoid blind spots that only they can see.

Resentment and anger towards another person poisons our soul, not theirs.

It is much wiser to know what you don't know than what you do know.

We are not in the results business. We are only in the action business.

Help the young see themselves with encouragement, positivity, and love. Their reflections often come from words of praise, support, and confidence building.

Gift giving is a wonderful expression of caring. The most precious gifts emanate from our hearts and don't require wrapping.

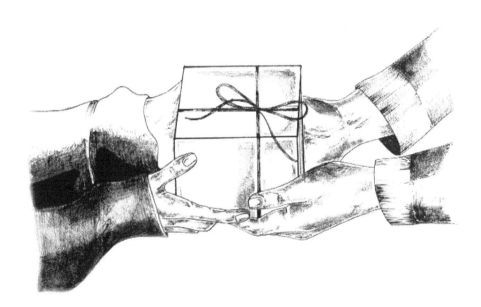

Don't take yourself so seriously. You are not that important in the universe anyway. Keeping a realistic perspective can provide balance in our emotional and spiritual wellness.

What the mind can conceive, the mind can achieve. Program your "human computer" with positive and constructive thoughts to achieve your very best.

Fear and worry deaden our spirit. Faith brings hope. Having faith requires a 24/7/365 consciousness of it. Good will always come out of the bad.

Human beings, similar to animals in the jungle, give off an "emotional" scent. That pheromone can either be of aggression, anger, peace or safety. What scent do you give off?

The real secret to navigating life's journey with greater ease is learning to be comfortable being uncomfortable.

Each decision we make during the course of our day requires making a choice that subtly impacts us. Your choices count more than you can imagine in your subconscious.

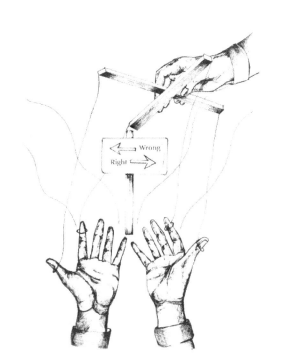

Hatred is an emotional drug. It intoxicates the soul and blinds rational behavior. The antidote is letting go of that poisonous emotional bondage.

Make deposits in your self-esteem account in lieu of your bank account. It builds greater riches.

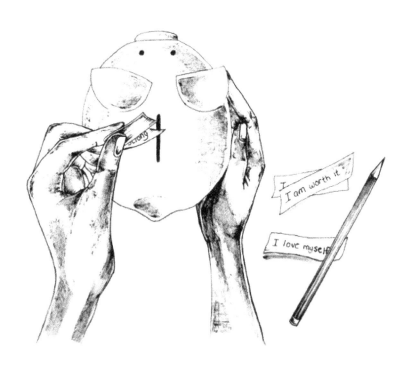

Each one of us has a natural rhythm which allows us to achieve our best performance. It is a lifetime effort to find our internal operating rhythm that supports our emotional, spiritual and physical being.

The most important language to use with children is the language of love.
Can you speak this language when you are upset with a child?

Our view of our problems gets diluted when we use the vastness of our universe as a backdrop. The more we comprehend this, the greater we realize how little our problems truly matter in the grand scheme of the universe.

What would you do if you were given too much change, or were not charged for something? The emotional price you pay costs far more than the value of the money. There is more spiritual value in imprinting in your subconscious the act of thoughtfulness and honesty.

Discarding clothing that you never wear is cathartic to avoid deluding ourself in thinking that there's a lot in our closet. This principle also applies to people in your life.

We were given the gift of life. We need to give something back as a way of passing on our blessings.

We always hurt the ones we love. Loved ones tend to be the easiest targets to injure. They shouldn't be the recipients of our unresolved emotions from a bad day at the office, a dispute with a friend, a flat tire or a long line at the store. They deserve our very best expressions of care and respect. We should resolve our emotions with the appropriate incident. Otherwise we create needless harm with our loved ones.

You are not the center of the universe and the stars and planets do not rotate around your axis. We are all shining stars revolving around in space.

We humans operate on an internal frequency like 98.6. There is a universe frequency which operates at a different frequency like 111.11. Tune in to the universal frequency through meditation to hear the latest news about yourself.

Giving is receiving. The value in giving transcends any material riches.

Happiness is a by-product of feeling comfortable in your own skin.
Happiness shines from the inside out.

Do these words ring true for you? Decent, appropriate, mindful, thoughtful, respectful, humane, intimate, considerate, even-tempered, stable, responsible, dependable, reliable, trustworthy and available. These are the merit badges of character given to those who join the highly esteemed human being troop.

When we ask for help from others and receive it, it is important to let that person know what has been accomplished from their advice. Putting a period at the end of this process is paying respect to your relationship and building a stronger bond.

An attitude of gratitude is the best medicine for a sick soul. Be grateful for what you have.

Human beings should always remember we are all in an iterative state throughout our lives. Mistakes will be made along on our journey of living and growing. It's how we learn right from wrong and good from bad.

Freedom is a by-product of letting go of the belief that we can control people, places and things. Staying in our own lane is the best solution.

Idle hands are the devil's playground, so the old saying goes. Another axiom offers a remedy: Move a muscle, change a thought.

Taking an olive in a store with a sign "Please do not sample our olives," is stealing. Your subconscious knows it's not right. It's so subtle that we can't see the effects until it adds up and these seemingly small things begin to affect our self-esteem.

Your work is just work. Don't give it life or make it your life. Making time for living in your workday is your real job.

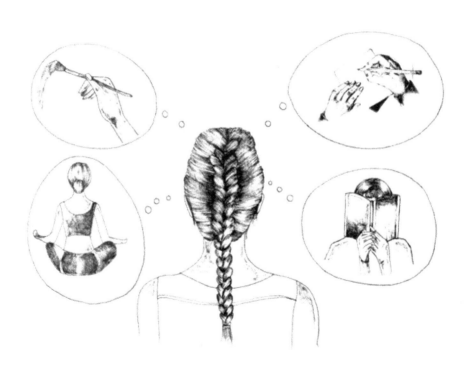

It takes a big person to say "I apologize." Do it soon after the incident. Time hardens our resolve to maintain the position we initially took.

Everyone deserves his or her place on this planet. Who am I to judge another?

If we are deceitful towards someone, we may find that our handiwork comes back to haunt us. Karma is a bitch!

Schools educate our children to provide them with knowledge and structure. Their environment, home life, community and friendships provide a basis to enrich and cultivate a quality life. As parents, our responsibility is to provide fertile soil so that these seedlings can bloom into beautiful, strong and bountiful people.

Traditions are markers along our journey of life. Like speed bumps in the road, traditions slow us down so we don't speed through life. Remembering to celebrate moments like birthdays, anniversaries and holidays are like dividers in our "book of life". He who dies with the most dividers wins.

Being able to laugh at yourself is the greatest sign of being comfortable with your humanity.

Don't wait to act on doing something that is important to you. You may lose interest by delaying, or the opportunity may pass you by. He who hesitates is lost!

Your job is a contract between you and your employer. You put in the work and at the end of each week you are paid. The contract is fulfilled, and you are both even. The level of our joy and enthusiasm about our work is an inverse proportion to the level of our expectations.

E is an important letter in the spiritual alphabet. E is for the effort in earning esteem. It can't be purchased, it can't be learned from a book or school. It can only be derived by doing estimable acts.

Breathing ten long, continuous, deep breaths is the simplest and easiest way to use your natural tranquillizer.

 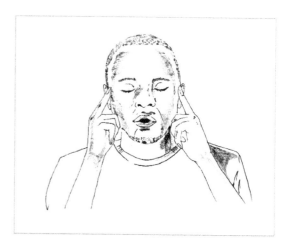

Let kids know that they can depend on you even when you are busy, angry or in discomfort. Kids may use "code" words to let you know that you are unavailable. Listen carefully for their "code."

Miracle-Gro only works for plants; There is no similar substance for human beings. Don't meddle with Mother Nature as she still works at her own pace. Be careful about trying to accelerate anything in your body, as the outcome may be counter to your health.

Throughout each day, there can be hundreds of seemingly insignificant encounters, choices and decisions. These positive or negative choices add up and get deposited into an emotional account. It's these little things that add up in building a solid character.

Letting someone else win an innocuous disagreement offers both harmony in the grand scheme of the relationship.

Do you bring out the best or the worst in people? If people really matter, then help them be their very best. Provide them with a feeling of caring, comfort and trust that their words are important. We all need to feel that we matter.

Jealousy and envy can distort our joy and zest for life. Striving for gratitude in all our affairs will ensure a heart and soul filled with love, tolerance and peace.

Most of us play movies in our heads. We should only run those movies which nurture or support our humanity. If a horror movie shows up, change the movie to one that offers happiness and peace.

We all need to take responsibility for our personal health and mental wellness. We cannot look to others to provide the emotional and physical surgery to improve the quality of our lives.

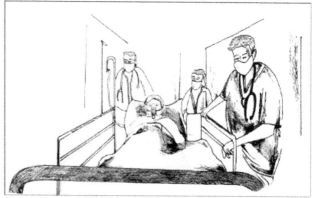

If you are doing your best, you will not have time to worry about failure. Look for good in all that happens to you, as good always comes out of the bad.

Our happiness is in inverse proportion to the level of our expectations.

Newton's third law states that "For every action, there is an opposite and equal reaction." Be mindful of your actions, as there is a force, Karma, that endeavors to balance things in the universe.

When offering advice, demonstrating by example provides the most lasting impact.

We us the term, "it's" overwhelming, "it's" making me upset, "it's driving me crazy and "it's" my spouse that's the problem. There is no "it!" We talk about "it" as if it is a force outside ourselves. Like this noxious force called "it" permeating our brain. It is our perception of reality that causes our feelings. You are responsible for your feelings, not "it!"

Breakups in relationships or partnerships require time to heal. We need to let people know that time is needed to rehabilitate emotionally and spiritually. Being vulnerable about that offers us a window of opportunity to rejuvenate ourselves.

All human beings need to consistently remember is that they are not a god or a higher power.

Our brain runs like a computer. We should only program into it, constructive and positive commands. Remember: garbage in, garbage out.

Power and emotional freedom comes from understanding that we are basically powerless over people and events. What we can do is express our feelings and let it go.

Live fully in the present moment since that's all that is real anyway. Everything else is an illusion. Yesterday is but a memory and tomorrow is yet unborn.

Financial riches are a by-product of smart thinking, hard work and perseverance. There is no free lunch.

Thank you for taking this journey with me.
Wishing you a life filled with health, peace,
and abundance.

Lightning Source UK Ltd.
Milton Keynes UK
UKHW032248190421
382261UK00007B/1128